STAR CATS

✦

A Feline Zodiac

LESLEY ANNE IVORY

LITTLE, BROWN AND COMPANY
BOSTON • NEW YORK • LONDON

INTRODUCTION

★

FOR centuries, for far longer than the human race has existed, cats have regarded the Heavens with contemplation and awe. They have basked in the Sun's warmth, sighed at the Moon, and marvelled at the stars.

Cats like to be unpredictable and the exception to every rule, so it is not always easy to guess under which of the twelve signs of the zodiac they were born.

There is no doubt that cats are aware of celestial influences. They feel their closest affinity with the Moon which, when it is at its fullest, evokes their most poetic and musical qualities. They adore the Sun too. Night or day, cats cannot lose – star-gazing by night, and sun-worshipping by day, they appreciate to the maximum extent the forces of warmth and mystery, exploiting them to their own particular advantage.

Whilst studying the characteristics and traits of the signs for this book, it has become amazingly clear to me how true most of us are to our sign's attributes. This applies not only to the human species, but certainly to every living thing born under the Sun. For me, especially with cats, whose natures I have loved and lived with for over half a century, and have observed in detail, it is remarkable to see how close they are to the behaviour predicted for each sign. I wonder whether, conversely, cats have studied us and, in matching us against our signs, have the last laugh? Were you to pass our home it is not inconceivable that you might hear a feline remark from Agneatha (our eldest) to her daughter, Motley, perhaps a comment on one of my shortcomings: 'Lesley can't help it – she's a Gemini, you know!'

The first publication of this book coincides with a year in which three major planets, Jupiter, Uranus, and Neptune, were in the sign of Aquarius, which some astrologers regard as signifying the beginning of a new age when mankind works for the good of Earth and its creatures. Let us pray so.

Kate's cat Sunshine, with the Temple of Apollo, Corinth, Greece.
In the borders, Sunshine's name appears in Greek, between the mosaic sun
roundels at the bottom, with that of Apollo above.

As the Sun passes through all the signs in the complete yearly cycle, it appears in various forms, in the top right-hand corner of every illustration. In the top left corner is the ruling planet and its sign, with the appropriate constellation and symbol of each sign shown either side of the top centre. In the bottom left-hand corner the related element is shown (Earth, Air, Fire, or Water), and at the bottom right is the associated gemstone. According to tradition, Aries appears first, because the Sun is in that constellation at the time of the Spring Equinox (although, due to the phenomenon of precession, it now appears in Pisces).

The various attributes of each sign shown within the illustrations and their borders are summarized at the end of the book. Such is the long history and complexity of the subject that accounts vary from authority to authority as to the dates, gems, colours, plants, and other affiliations, so while those I have depicted are generally accepted, there may be some disparities.

Those of you who have met my cats in my previous books will find a number of old friends here, as well as the cats of my friends, together representing each of the twelve signs. They appear not only on their respective pages, but also – along with many other creatures – elsewhere in the paintings. The front cover depicts Motley (with Gabby and Twiglet in miniature), while within Virgo I have shown Gemma, Muppet, Emu, Agneatha and Mintaka (his début appearance), and not forgetting Tassel the dog; Leo includes a prehistoric insect trapped in amber; in Cancer, along with Malteazer, there are snails and a tortoise, while Scorpio has a hidden spider. As well as these animals, I have included a huge range of related flowers, herbs and other plants, and shown more than 3,700 gems – there are 900 in Scorpio alone.

The settings for the paintings are based on themes that have been inspired by art as diverse as Egyptian, Roman, Arabic, Celtic, Medieval, and Art Nouveau. To achieve authenticity in these and in their astrological features, I have consulted numerous books and done an enormous amount of research in museums, especially the British Museum and the Metropolitan Museum, New York. To these sources, and everyone who has helped me with this book, I wish to extend my warmest thanks.

Lesley Anne Ivory

Mintaka learning about the stars from his mother Lucy.
Mintaka is named after the third star in Orion's Belt, the constellation seen
here above Lucy's head, with the comet Hale-Bopp at the top.

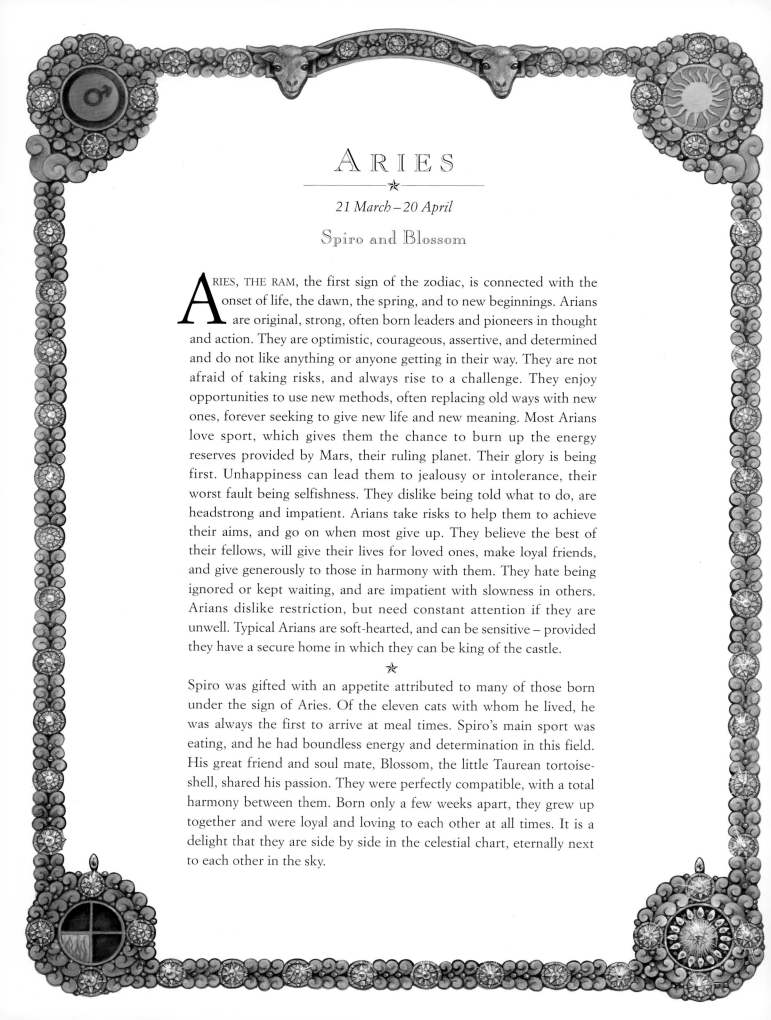

ARIES

✸

21 March – 20 April

Spiro and Blossom

ARIES, THE RAM, the first sign of the zodiac, is connected with the onset of life, the dawn, the spring, and to new beginnings. Arians are original, strong, often born leaders and pioneers in thought and action. They are optimistic, courageous, assertive, and determined and do not like anything or anyone getting in their way. They are not afraid of taking risks, and always rise to a challenge. They enjoy opportunities to use new methods, often replacing old ways with new ones, forever seeking to give new life and new meaning. Most Arians love sport, which gives them the chance to burn up the energy reserves provided by Mars, their ruling planet. Their glory is being first. Unhappiness can lead them to jealousy or intolerance, their worst fault being selfishness. They dislike being told what to do, are headstrong and impatient. Arians take risks to help them to achieve their aims, and go on when most give up. They believe the best of their fellows, will give their lives for loved ones, make loyal friends, and give generously to those in harmony with them. They hate being ignored or kept waiting, and are impatient with slowness in others. Arians dislike restriction, but need constant attention if they are unwell. Typical Arians are soft-hearted, and can be sensitive – provided they have a secure home in which they can be king of the castle.

✸

Spiro was gifted with an appetite attributed to many of those born under the sign of Aries. Of the eleven cats with whom he lived, he was always the first to arrive at meal times. Spiro's main sport was eating, and he had boundless energy and determination in this field. His great friend and soul mate, Blossom, the little Taurean tortoise-shell, shared his passion. They were perfectly compatible, with a total harmony between them. Born only a few weeks apart, they grew up together and were loyal and loving to each other at all times. It is a delight that they are side by side in the celestial chart, eternally next to each other in the sky.

TAURUS

★

21 April – 21 May

Gemma

Taureans are patient, solid, and reliable, strong in body and mind and in the face of difficulties, but need emotional security themselves above all. They are positive thinkers and peace-loving; their secret fear is being disturbed from this peace. Taureans love open-air life and contact with the soil, and are often horticulturists or keen gardeners. They enjoy good food and are often excellent cooks. They show warmth and affection towards their friends and expect them to be dependable and unchanging too. Taureans are slow to anger unless really provoked, but under tensions their normal patience sometimes gives way to sudden rushes of temper. Those born under the sign of Taurus love to be praised, make loving and loyal partners, and caring, attentive parents. They enjoy their leisure hours, are often musical, and can enjoy wasting time. Taureans set out to achieve the best in life, their motto being 'the best in life is worth waiting for'. And being tenacious, they get it.

★

Gemma has many of the more praiseworthy attributes of Taureans, and eyes of emerald – the colour of the Taurean gemstone. She is peaceful and patient, has a natural charm of her own, and loves all beauteous things. She made the most loving and attentive mother to her four little Leo-born kittens, and is especially warm and affectionate to us, her human family. She infinitely prefers our company to that of our other feline residents, because no peace threats come from us, and in us she has her necessary security. She has the Taurean steady gaze, and loves the garden, spending hours of happiness amongst the leaves and flowers.

GEMINI

22 May – 21 June

Christie and Zelly

OFTEN called the butterflies of the zodiac, typical Geminis are charming, sensitive, youthful, and friendly spirits. They are adaptable, and merge and adjust easily, restlessly flitting in and out of varied moods, rarely satisfied in their curiosity about life. They are the great communicators of the zodiac, and love to talk. A Gemini has a twin personality, a double-sided nature: one witty and charming, the other sullen and pessimistic. They can change from one extreme to the other in a flash. Those born under the sign of Gemini are likely to hold two different points of view on everything. They can be manipulative and crafty in bending the truth, and as cunning as monkeys. They take nothing seriously, and are light-hearted and flirtatious. Their movements are usually quick and active. Having highly-strung nervous systems, tensions can build up. Never dull, they have a childlike demand for attention. They forever seek wide-ranging fresh mental stimulation – their biggest fear is being bored, and every minute must be filled with activity to burn off surplus energy. They are fun to be with – if you can stand the pace! They enjoy company, but have little time for leisure. They retain their youth usually longer than those born under any other sign, simply having no time to grow old. Life is a game that must be ever full of variety and fresh interests, free from routine. Geminis constantly search for their twin soul mate in life, and have a deep need for emotional warmth and kindness.

Christie and Zelly, who are twin girls, are typical of those born under this sign. They are inquisitive, chatty, can be annoying, never settle, and flit around like butterflies – although they actually prefer collecting moths and spiders. They are always together: Zelly is the great communicator, and always first, with Christie just a step behind, and slightly quieter. They both love attention and give me a wonderful greeting whenever I visit their cottage, peering into my basket to see what I have brought them. They like to be in symmetry with each other, often posing like bookends on the arm of their sofa.

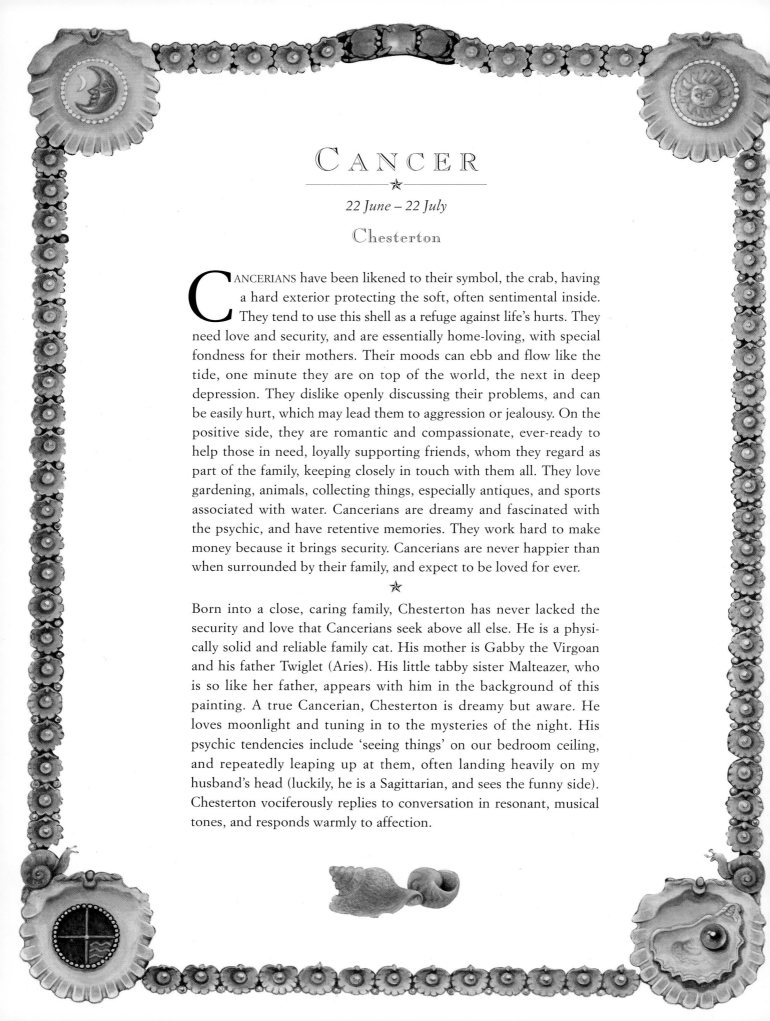

CANCER

★

22 June – 22 July

Chesterton

CANCERIANS have been likened to their symbol, the crab, having a hard exterior protecting the soft, often sentimental inside. They tend to use this shell as a refuge against life's hurts. They need love and security, and are essentially home-loving, with special fondness for their mothers. Their moods can ebb and flow like the tide, one minute they are on top of the world, the next in deep depression. They dislike openly discussing their problems, and can be easily hurt, which may lead them to aggression or jealousy. On the positive side, they are romantic and compassionate, ever-ready to help those in need, loyally supporting friends, whom they regard as part of the family, keeping closely in touch with them all. They love gardening, animals, collecting things, especially antiques, and sports associated with water. Cancerians are dreamy and fascinated with the psychic, and have retentive memories. They work hard to make money because it brings security. Cancerians are never happier than when surrounded by their family, and expect to be loved for ever.

★

Born into a close, caring family, Chesterton has never lacked the security and love that Cancerians seek above all else. He is a physically solid and reliable family cat. His mother is Gabby the Virgoan and his father Twiglet (Aries). His little tabby sister Malteazer, who is so like her father, appears with him in the background of this painting. A true Cancerian, Chesterton is dreamy but aware. He loves moonlight and tuning in to the mysteries of the night. His psychic tendencies include 'seeing things' on our bedroom ceiling, and repeatedly leaping up at them, often landing heavily on my husband's head (luckily, he is a Sagittarian, and sees the funny side). Chesterton vociferously replies to conversation in resonant, musical tones, and responds warmly to affection.

LEO

★

23 July – 23 August

Octopussy and Motley

TYPICAL Leos are positive people, dignified and sunny-natured, their movements cat-like, with heads held proudly high. They are perfectionists: only the best is good enough, and they will work hard to achieve it. They aim to be top, king of all they survey, and expect to be leader, and treated like royalty. Leos are honest, loyal and trusting, and presume the same of others. Being born directors, their natural enthusiasm leads many into politics, teaching, or managerial occupations. Leos are among the foremost wildlife conservationists, specially caring for the Big Cats. Their need for power can make them bossy and domineering. They should try to guard against vanity and intolerance. Leos' worst fault is that they assume they know best. They have great courage and strength in a crisis, often take risks, and work well under pressure. Leos have a good sense of dress and style, and entertain friends generously. They love sport and exercise, recharging their energies through love, on which they depend and without which they become depressed. Unhappy Leos can be easily hurt, and become arrogant or sulky. As long as they are loved they can cope.

★

Octopussy and Motley are true Leos, extrovert, loving, and playful. Motley, Octopussy's sister, is over-generous with her love for humans, but is jealous of other cats. She expects our love to be just for her, and then she's happy. She warmly welcomes our visitors, and lovingly helps entertain them. She insists she knows best, despite our occasional protests, but although easily hurt by reprimands, she chooses to persist, without sulking for too long. Leonine majestic Octopussy dreams of kingship, rather attempting to achieve the position by force. He has cause to be proud, and having been declared to be the most famous tabby Leo in the world, expects to remain so. Octopussy and Motley are certainly loved, which provides them with the necessary power contentedly to reign above us.

VIRGO

★

24 August – 22 September

Gabrielle (Gabby)

VIRGO is a complex sign. Virgoans are still waters that run deep, whose nervous turbulence is often hidden beneath a mask of security. They are amusing, modest, and sympathetic, but fussy. Being too involved with little details, they often neglect the main issue. Their aim is self perfection, and they mostly direct their worst faults, criticizing and complaining, towards themselves. They are health and hygiene fanatics, and like to be prepared for all events with a variety of remedies in their medicine cupboards. They possess good colour sense, enjoy home management, gardening and flowers, domestic pets, books and crafts, and keeping busy making things to occupy their practical, intelligent minds. Content to be on their own, Virgoans dislike noise or crowds.

Gabby, the sleek feline maiden, has Virgoan modesty, charm, and immense underlying intelligence. She uses quietly persistent techniques relentlessly to gain her own way. One of her more annoying habits is seriously hindering her owner's solving of crosswords by masking the clues with her velvety hind quarters. Fastidiously colour conscious, she colour codes wherever possible. Always on black, no matter where or what it is, she can be found curled up on expensive silk jackets, or having forty winks on a black plastic bag. Typically cautious about making committed partnerships, three years elapsed before she married Twiglet, the Arian, and had their dear little Cancerian kittens, Chesterton and Malteazer, in our wardrobe. Always aware, she is suddenly at your side if you need her, emanating beneficial warmth until you feel better. She tunes into the atmosphere from a vantage point in the kitchen. You may not know what she is thinking, but, above all, you do know that she cares.

LIBRA

✴

23 September – 23 October

Clea and Lily

LIBRANS need balance and justice, and seek harmonious relation-ships. They thrive amongst those who are undemanding and supportive. Librans are kind, self-controlled, practised in the arts of diplomacy, and make charming hosts. Their fear is being alone, although they will nearly always disguise the fact, and keep a calm personal appearance. They are good listeners and conversation-alists, but dislike heated arguments. Although seldom angry, short bursts of temper may arise if provoked. They hate criticism or pres-sure. Librans can be indecisive: being peacemakers they usually see both sides of a dispute, and are then incapable of reaching a decision either way. They are likely to be involved in law, politics, or diplo-macy. Librans are intelligent, appreciate the arts, and relaxing in tasteful surroundings. They are not keen on excessive exercise and sometimes tend towards extravagance.

✴

Clea and Lily are sisters, and live with artist Dana in London. They are a well mannered, companionable pair, with loving dispositions, and enjoy a leisurely life in their artistic home. They seem to relish art, and posing for paintings. It is unclear whether or not they are into politics, but they do have leanings towards the law, and are very interested in justice. Having very just attitudes towards each other, Clea and Lily have to cope with a renegade fellow resident called Dumpling, who has no sense of justice at all, which at times brings out the less favourable, resentful traits of Libran behaviour. They certainly prefer company to being alone, and conduct harmonious conversations with those they know.

SCORPIO

★

24 October – 22 November

Sirius

TYPICAL Scorpios have boundless energy and strong constitutions. They are determined, caring, compulsive, and completely unshockable. They are always investigating, loving to clarify what is obscure, delving into the heart of the matter, often seeking hidden meanings. Many possess a sixth sense. They dislike being analysed, and cannot bear to think others know more than they do. They are courageous and remain unruffled in all situations. They will do anything to help others, but beware the sting in the tail if they don't like you. Many a more timid person has recoiled from the glare of a Scorpio's intense eyes. They thrive on activity, having too much vitality to enjoy relaxation. Scorpios usually become deeply attached to one person and dominate them, and are said to be in harmony with Capricorns. Their great aspiration is to learn the meaning of compassionate love.

Sirius, the Singapurra, is extremely demanding, constantly seeking out attention, incredibly affectionate, and thrives on love. He expects to get his own way with the three other cats with whom he lives, forcibly commandeering chairs, and sitting on the occupants if they don't give way. Telephones excite him: immediately one rings, he searches it out, knocks off the receiver, and presses the buttons. One phone had to be hidden inside the bread bin and taped down, and still he found it, and got in. He is fear-free – as the other cats flee the vacuum cleaner, he will try to ride it. He is the one who enthusiastically watches thunderstorms, while the others are trembling beneath the table. He is fascinated by anything that does not belong to him, and cannot bear to miss anything. When playing he can be rough, but he is never spiteful; unlike the Scorpion, there is no sting in his tail. He sleeps with his owner Carina, draped over her head like earphones, while Muggley the Capricorn slips under her duvet, hoping he hasn't noticed.

SAGITTARIUS

★

23 November – 21 December

Ra Ra

SAGITTARIUS is the sign of the Heavenly Archer. Travel and freedom are essential to the happy Sagittarian, the zodiac's wanderers, forever either travelling physically, or exploring the mind's horizons. They are naturally optimistic, but extremely restless; not everything they start gets completed, so impatient are they to move on. The most fortunate and likeable of all the signs, they attract many friends with their warmth, understanding, and good humour. Being open-minded and frank, they often appear tactless, but they never mean to hurt. Sagittarians are uncomplaining and dependable, and have a close affinity with nature, particularly being attracted towards dogs and horses. They will become bored without a challenge. Their mental ability is above average; learning new languages is an ideal quest. Active, often risky sports like horse- or motor-racing are perfect outlets. Their aim is to discover the meaning of existence, and consequently religion and philosophy are often significant in their lives. They are hungry for knowledge and have good memories for facts, but may have a tendency to preach.

Ra Ra is an exception to the rule, and – apart from his restless vitality and lack of tact – quite untrue to his sign. Hyperactive, with teeth to match, he will recycle his blankets overnight just to keep his mind alive, then is totally amazed that we are unimpressed with his efforts. He loves people but is impatient towards cats born under supposedly harmonious signs, and he can't stand dogs or horses. Also unlike true Sagittarians he enjoys the occasional fracas, and hurling arrow-sharp, menacing miaows at innocent Leos. Perhaps he lacks sufficient physical travel, and we can only guess where he travels in his mind, but the language he uses is loud, complaining, and obstinately incessant until he is given what he wants. Where food is concerned he is the only Sagittarian in the world whose main fault is greed. As far as human feelings towards him are concerned, he is beautiful, annoying, exasperating, and loveable, but ask Octopussy what he thinks, and there hangs a completely different tale.

CAPRICORN

22 December – 20 January

Muggley

GREAT potential lies within every Capricorn. They are practical, sincere, and studious, but this is the sign of contrasts, and their changing temperaments may well affect their ambitions. Capricorns are worriers, their moods, suddenly varying for no apparent reason, ranging through capriciousness to melancholy, warmth to cold reserve, while from pessimistic grumbling, dry humour can suddenly burst through the gloom. They tend to believe they know best, have critical views, and are easily depressed. Capricorns hate to be teased or made to feel foolish. By defeating the negative they gradually achieve the heights with determination and hard work. Capricorns detest pressure, and prefer to work at a distance from others. They enjoy research and books. They yearn for security and love, aim to understand others' feelings, and never forsake friends. Fresh air and relaxing with music best restores their spirits.

Young Capricorns often look older than their years. Muggley the Cornish Rex gives the impression of being an old man, when in fact he is quite young. From an extremely lively kitten he matured into a serious, sensitive cat who likes his comforts. He is long-suffering and needs special times of quiet attention with his owner. Since the arrival of Sirius the Scorpio he finds himself somewhat pushed around. He always gives way, and never stands up for himself by retaliating. Muggley likes to maintain his dignity, is an anxious cat, and easily upset if made to look silly. Being usually small-framed, Capricornean shapeliness relies on exercise. As Muggley does not believe in strenuous exercise, and seriously enjoys his food, his vet advised dieting – he wasn't overweight, just in need of toning. He and Sirius live with journalist Carina, and two other cats. They assist her in the office, Sirius helping her type, while Muggley sits inactively on a hot radiator watching her with a concerned eye.

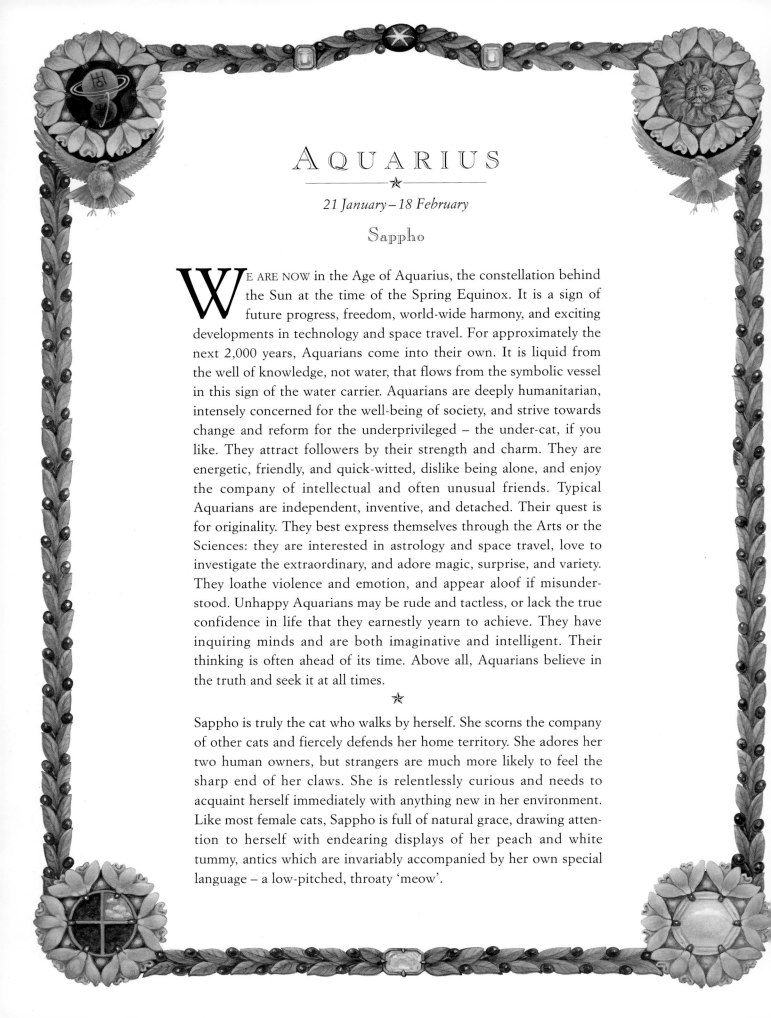

AQUARIUS

★

21 January – 18 February

Sappho

WE ARE NOW in the Age of Aquarius, the constellation behind the Sun at the time of the Spring Equinox. It is a sign of future progress, freedom, world-wide harmony, and exciting developments in technology and space travel. For approximately the next 2,000 years, Aquarians come into their own. It is liquid from the well of knowledge, not water, that flows from the symbolic vessel in this sign of the water carrier. Aquarians are deeply humanitarian, intensely concerned for the well-being of society, and strive towards change and reform for the underprivileged – the under-cat, if you like. They attract followers by their strength and charm. They are energetic, friendly, and quick-witted, dislike being alone, and enjoy the company of intellectual and often unusual friends. Typical Aquarians are independent, inventive, and detached. Their quest is for originality. They best express themselves through the Arts or the Sciences: they are interested in astrology and space travel, love to investigate the extraordinary, and adore magic, surprise, and variety. They loathe violence and emotion, and appear aloof if misunderstood. Unhappy Aquarians may be rude and tactless, or lack the true confidence in life that they earnestly yearn to achieve. They have inquiring minds and are both imaginative and intelligent. Their thinking is often ahead of its time. Above all, Aquarians believe in the truth and seek it at all times.

★

Sappho is truly the cat who walks by herself. She scorns the company of other cats and fiercely defends her home territory. She adores her two human owners, but strangers are much more likely to feel the sharp end of her claws. She is relentlessly curious and needs to acquaint herself immediately with anything new in her environment. Like most female cats, Sappho is full of natural grace, drawing attention to herself with endearing displays of her peach and white tummy, antics which are invariably accompanied by her own special language – a low-pitched, throaty 'meow'.

PISCES

✭

19 February – 20 March

Angel

PISCEANS, the most psychic and spiritual of all the signs, are strongly attracted to mysticism and the unknown, and are highly receptive to atmosphere. They are true Samaritans and never refuse to help those in need. Compassionate and sensitive to others' feelings, they live and act in their companions' interests. To succeed, they must swim with the tide of life, using their positive side. Escaping troubles or reality by transcending into a personal fantasy world can lead to failure. They need love, which vitalizes them; without it they have difficulty in coping with problems. Pisceans love acting, happily hiding behind another's character, and find peace in music and poetry.

✭

Angel has never quite forgotten her unfortunate experiences in kittenhood with a teasing baby at her first home. Even now, after several years with us, she considers discipline a threat, and in resisting it may bite, in pure self-defence (we had already named her before we learned her ways). She is very happy and docile when relaxed, and needs love and attention, but only on her own terms. She will slide softly onto your lap and smile as you stroke her silky warm fur, then suddenly nip you when enough is enough. Left alone she quickly calms and gives you a lick. She prefers company to being alone, and spends ages playing rough games with her friend, Dandelion – the flower of the name being a Piscean attribute. Angel is friendly and sociable and often waits on the garden wall for attention from passers-by, which she usually gets. She likes freedom and variety, and revels in situations that involve risk or have a slight element of danger. She is also a dreamer, and escapes into her fantasy world whilst gazing out of the bathroom window. She is keenly interested in pond life and water lilies, and enjoys water sports providing she doesn't get wet. Her appetite is phenomenal – she could happily exist on seafood and biscuits.

Aries

Ruling planet: Mars
Element: Fire
Gemstones: Diamond, Garnet
Spices: Capers, Red chilli, Mustard seeds
Plants: Honeysuckle, Bryony, Cowslip, Hops, Thistle
Herbs: Basil, Garlic, Mint, Rosemary
Vegetables: Leek, Onion
Tree: Hawthorn
Colour: Red

The globe is inspired by a celestial globe in the
Metropolitan Museum, New York. The Aries sign is based
on the *Belles Heures of Jean duc de Berry* (c.1406–09). The
floor is taken from a medieval tiled pavement.

Taurus

Ruling planet: Venus
Element: Earth
Gemstones: Emerald, Topaz
Fruit: Pear, Apple, Apricot
Spices: Mixed spices
Plants: Dog rose, Mallow, Violet, Daisy
Herb: Thyme
Crops: Wheat, Grapes
Colours: Pastel shades

The background is taken from a 2nd-century AD Egyptian
mummy case, and the Sun disc from a 9th-century BC
Babylonian tablet, both in the British Museum. The
Egytian gold bull (664–380 BC) is in the Theodore M. Davis
Collection, Metropolitan Museum, New York.

Gemini

Ruling planet: Mercury
Element: Air
Gemstones: Garnet, Tiger's eye
Fruit: Nuts – Hazelnut, Horse chestnut
Plants: Lavender, Fern, Maidenhair fern, Lily of the Valley
Herbs: Dill, Marjoram
Vegetable: Peas
Colours: Yellow, Love of all colours (rainbow)
Animals: Hyacinth macaw, Monkey

The sign derives from the Waltham Abbey zodiac ceiling.
Based on a 13th-century pattern, it was designed by William
Burges and painted by Edward Poynter in the 1860s.

Cancer

Ruling planet: Moon
Element: Water
Gemstones: Pearl, Moonstone
Spices: Coriander, Nutmeg
Flowers: Moonwort, Lily, Saxifrage, Convolvulus,
Purslane, Cow parsley
Tree: Laurel
Herb: Balm
Vegetable/fungus: Cabbage, Mushroom
Colours: Soft greys, Blues, Silver
Animals: Tortoise, Snail

The Cancer sign is from an English psalter from
York, c.1170. The Sun disc is inspired by a German
illuminated manuscript of c.1490.

Leo

Ruling planet: Sun
Element: Fire
Gemstones: Ruby, Amber
Fruit: Citrus, Almond
Spice: Frankincense
Plants: Chamomile, Orchid, Sunflower, Marigold,
Celandine, Passion flower
Herbs: Bay, Rue, Rosemary
Vegetable: Watercress
Crops: Grapes, Rice
Colours: Yellow, Orange
Animals: Lion, Bee

The background is of a bay tree with hives and 19th-century
tiles from Dartmouth, Devon. The embossed and incised
gold lions and vine relief is inspired by one from Mycenae
dating from the second half of the 16th century BC. The gold
disc represents Shamash the Sun God. The terracotta lion
water spout is based on a Greek original.

Virgo

Ruling planet: Mercury
Element: Earth
Gemstones: Opal, Peridot, Sardonyx
Spices: Cardamom, Caraway, Aniseed
Flowers: Narcissus, Cat's ear, Forget-me-not, Buttercup
Trees: Oak, Hazel
Herbs: Fennel, Sage
Vegetable: Carrot
Colours: Green, Dark brown, Navy
Animals: Domestic pets – Dog, Cat

The Virgo sign is taken from Harley 4940, a manuscript in
the British Library. The background and tiles are inspired by
13th-century medieval decorative art. The oak and hazel
details come from a medieval gittern (a guitar-like instrument).

LIBRA

Ruling planet: Venus
Element: Air
Gemstones: Jade, Emerald
Fruit: Soft berries – Strawberry, Raspberry, Blackberry
Plants: Daffodil, Bluebell, Foxglove, Rose
Trees: Ash, Poplar
Herbs: Parsley, Mint
Crops and spices: Most cereals, Spices, Beans
Colours: Pink, Pale green, Blues
Animals: Snake, Lizard

The Libra sign is inspired by a 16th-century woodcut. The snake and lizard come from a medieval bestiary. The scales are Greek – they are balanced when the birds' beaks meet.

SCORPIO

Ruling planet: Pluto (formerly Mars)
Element: Water
Gemstones: Turquoise, Opal
Spice: Ginger
Flowers: Briar, Honeysuckle, Geranium, Thistle, Hibiscus
Tree: Hawthorn
Cactus: Pheasant-tail aloe
Herbs: Witch hazel, Catmint
Vegetable: Onion
Colours: Deep red, Maroon, Black, Blue-green
Animals: Grey lizard, Wolf

The background is taken from 16th-century Arabic designs. The Sun is a detail from a piece of 17th-century Indian cotton. The scarab beetles are inspired by ancient Egyptian jewellery.

SAGITTARIUS

Ruling planet: Jupiter
Element: Fire
Gemstones: Lapis lazuli, Topaz
Fruit: Bilberry, Fig, Mulberry, Rhubarb
Spices: Cinnamon, Clove
Flowers: Houseleek, Carnation, Borage, Rushes
Vegetables: Garlic, Celery
Colours: Blue, Royal blue, Rich purple, White
Animals: Deer, Horse

The sign and the zodiac circle are inspired by the work of the Art Nouveau artist Alphonse Mucha (1860–1939).

CAPRICORN

Ruling planet: Saturn
Element: Earth
Gemstones: Amethyst, Turquoise
Flowers: Knapweed, Hemlock, Deadly nightshade
Trees: Ivy, Holly, Pine, Beech, Yew
Vegetables: Potato, Beet
Crop: Barley
Colours: Dark brown, Green, Grey, Black, Indigo, Violet
Animal: Goat

The borders are inspired by two Celtic masterpieces, the *Lindisfarne Gospels* and the *Book of Kells*, and the Capricorn sign by one in an early English psalter. The cat's face at the bottom centre is from a 1st-century AD bowl handle in the National Museum of Wales, Cardiff. The setting is Wheal Kitty, a tin mine in Celtic Cornwall.

AQUARIUS

Ruling planet: Uranus (formerly Saturn)
Element: Air
Gemstones: Aquamarine, Star sapphire, Sapphire
Spices: Black pepper, Chilli
Flowers: Orchid, Solomon's seal, Snowdrop, Pansy
Trees: Olive, Apple blossom
Crop: Barley
Vegetables: Spinach, Parsnip
Fruit: Star fruit
Birds: Eagle, Albatross, Peacock
Colours: Violet, Electric blue, Turquoise, Silver grey

The sign is based on a 4th-century AD Roman mosaic found at Hammath, near Tiberius, Israel. The vessel and Sun motif are from the Roman baths at Bath.

PISCES

Ruling planet: Neptune (formerly Jupiter)
Element: Water
Gemstones: Moonstone and Bloodstone
Fruit: Lime, Melon
Vegetable: Cucumber
Plants: Moss, Palm
Spices: Nutmeg, Star aniseed
Flowers: Dandelion, Water lily
Colour: Soft sea green

The Pisces sign comes from the *Belles Heures of Jean duc de Berry* (c.1406–09). The background is a mosaic from Pompeii, now in the Museo Nazionale, Naples.

To Chris Beetles, with love, Star.

*Dandelion and Lalande's Cat. In 1799 the French astronomer Joseph Jérôme Le Français
de Lalande (1732–1807) added a thirty-fourth animal constellation to the night sky – a cat,
Felis, which he located between Hydra and Antlia Pneumatica (the air pump).
Sadly, it disappeared from subsequent star atlases.*

*The Zodiac wheel on the title page depicts Aries (top, centre) with Spiro; Pisces/Angel;
Aquarius/Sappho; Capricorn/Muggley; Sagittarius/Ra Ra; Scorpio/Sirius; Libra/Clea;
Virgo/Gabby; Leo/Motley; Cancer/Chesterton; Gemini/Christie and Zelly; Taurus/Gemma.*

Illustrations copyright © by Lesley Anne Ivory, 1998
Licensed by Copyrights

First Edition

ISBN 0 316 88221 6

A CIP catalogue for this book is available
from the British Library

Conceived, edited and designed by Ash and Higton

Little, Brown and Company (UK)
Brettenham House
Lancaster Place
London WC2E 7EN

PRINTED AND BOUND IN ITALY